SCRIBBLES

Debi Bhaumik

Copyright © 2021 by Debi Bhaumik
All rights reserved. This book or any portion thereof may not be reproduced or used in any manner whatsoever without the express written permission of the respective writer of the respective poem/story except for the use of brief quotations in a book review. The writers of the respective works hold sole responsibility of the originality of the poems/stories and The Write Order is not responsible in any way whatsoever.

Printed in India

ISBN: 978-93-5565-021-4

First Printing, 2022

The Write Order

Koramangala, Bangalore

Karnataka- 560029

THE WRITE ORDER PUBLICATIONS.

www.thewriteorder.com

Dedication

"Remembering you is easy,

missing you the hardest.....

Love you Baba"

Table of Contents

She......The Warrior	10
Apostles of Dreams	13
Closer	22
Emerging You	25
A Song Of Past	30
A Love Story	34
With You	39
Forever You Are Mine	42
Woman As You Are	46
An Absence In Chaos	50
La Vie Magnifique	55
A Golden Reward	60
Men Dream At Sea	63

A Masterpiece	68
A Soul Within	72
Night Falls	76

She......The Warrior

"She was afraid of heights

But she was much more afraid of never flying"

- Atticus

The dawn showed a flamingo sky...

It was time to say goodbye

Rose she from the arms of her warrior

Strained with memories of love...

The rains swept across the sea

The waters where the enemy would be

Awaiting the dawn for her warrior

Who lay yet unharmed...

She crept low to the porch

Where ashes spread from the nights flaming

torch

Reminding her of ignited passions

The rains brought in last night...

Now she stands watching the grey beyond

One more day...

once more if she could bond

The warmth of breath ...

the embrace so bold

Endearing intimacy...

the besotted delight...

Her warrior must leave and bid adieu

The vibrant pennant the winds that blew

The bugle voiced the final call

She watched in calm her warrior's eyes...

They embraced each other one last time

Under the sky filled with battle chime

He held her close...

embraced her long

As she knew in her heart she felt him no

more...

Apostles of Dreams

If I had wings, I would fly where eagles dare to tread.....

With you on my back, in a spur of a moment gliding through the wet-dry clouds, slicing the wind to escalate the highest......

And see the world from there....

The ravines....

Meandering rivers....

Snow capped mountains that stand mighty proud.....

You would, as usual, say in an uneasy way....

To leave and get back to the ground....

I would hug you,

Embrace you, till the time you forget the

obvious.....

None to see us here....

Rest my head on your shoulder .....

Yours on mine....

Then in a magical moment, sprinkle the pixie

dust to reach the serene Chandrataal lake.....

The full moon dips at the lake on the darkest

night when the spotless sky reveals it's true

black against a milky white, ash stained,

imperfect moon.....

Standing in the water, waist deep, looking
deeper into your eyes, my hands around your
neck, yours around mine.....

You would, as usual, say in an uneasy way.......
To leave and get back to the ground....
I would hug you,.
Embrace you till the time you forget the
obvious.....
None to see us here....Kiss your face
With a twist, Harry's broken wand will spin and
roll over among the sands of Pharaohs......

Against the twilight of the dusky morning, the shimmering triads hopelessly trying to make a shadow in the sands of time...... Giggling while we roll on the soft warm sand....
breathing up heaved on your face yours on mine....
The Phoenix guarding over our head.....
You would as usual say in an uneasy way.......
To leave n get back to the ground....
i would hug you.....
Embrace you till the time you forgot the obvious....
none to see us here.....
Engage your lips with all the passion

A clap in the hand and clicking the heels of
Bhooter raja shoes shall run laughing ...among
the upper slopes of Rhine in to the dense
foliage....Hiking our way hand in hand slipping
through all slopes the chill on your back
warmth in our hearts hugging with much
yearning....

Where the noon sun plays a hide n seek
through the canopy of leaves glistening against
the white Crystal snow on the highest branches
of Scots pines oaks elm....
Where once the Grimm fairy tales the ghostly

Vikings wrote ....

you would as usual say in an uneasy way.......

To leave n get back to the ground....

i would hug you......

Embrace you till the time you forgot the

obvious......

none to see us here......

Pulling you closer taking you in my arms me in

yours engaging once more ....

Shaking the genie in a bottle command to take

us to ground......

The ground where you would stand....

and I lie low......

6 feet under......

The ground as you wished….

As I wished..….

The fluttering hearts now apart.…

None to see…

The eye of Phoenix.…

The haunting Grimm brothers.…

The scourging eagle eyes nor the light of the imperfectly perfect full moon shall not reach us now..….

Yearning from beneath whispering your name till the last shall deliver you the ground.…

At ease now ….

None to see us..….

Ever again.…

Love you.…

Closer

Showers hit the pane high and low....

The clinking patters play

Not so long ago was I next to him.....

For the fragrance still lasts away.

To him it was playful.....

Glinting eyes yet to see

And yet the question lingers.....

Why were you closer to me?

The glasses, dark and deep....

Hid the glint away

Did you not feel the skin...

The throbbing heart swayed.

Where were you my friend.....

Close to me yet so far

The fluttering emotions....

Doors to the soul left ajar.

The silent touch...

up heaved emotions.....

The hand held warm and cold

And yet the question lingers....

Are you not told?

Demanding as I am....

Would brave heart the true....

The clocks are ticking by......

Closer....

closest to you.

Emerging You

A usual happy life

A morning bright and blue

Have you ever met yourself

Emerging across you?

Among the worldly conversations

That raise your spirits and hue

Have you ever met yourself

Emerging across you?

In the mirror that you see in modest

admiration

A reflection you thought you knew

Have you ever met yourself

Emerging across you?

When you lay watching the stars

Matching imagination that your fingers drew

Have you ever met yourself

Emerging across you?

In the arms that you hide, unmistakably warm

A sense of one that grew

Have you ever met yourself

Emerging across you?

The rains of emotions that quenches the soul

At night when the humdrum had bid adieu

Have you ever met yourself

Emerging across you?

In the besotting silence of a love so deep

Where you swam to rinse and bathe anew

Have you ever met yourself

Emerging across you?

As in the eyes of a complete love

Where the world in you, he view

Have you ever met yourself

Emerging across you?

A Song of Past

The train left the station

The whistles blew off guard

Unmindful in my journey

I hummed a song of the past

The song of love and joy

Of closeness and memories amassed

Unmindful in my journey

I hummed a song of the past

The fields ran green and brooks ran blue

Yellow dandelions showered a contrast

Unmindful in my journey

I hummed a song of the past

The song rose high on one of the souls

The warm embrace that did outlast

Unmindful in my journey

I hummed a song of the past

The beauty of the lips that kissed with zeal

The sailor's heart dis-mast

Unmindful in my journey

I hummed a song of the past

The rain quenched the country hill

As the train looped the hillocks cast

Unmindful in my journey

I hummed a song of the past

The end of journey on a hill...cottages that run

afar

The closing twilight that spoke avast

Unmindful through my journey

I hummed the song of the past

A Love Story

"She walks in beauty, like the night

Of cloudless climes

And starry skies"

-Lord Byron

She was born a beauty of the realms

A child who played and sang

Of meadows past across the field

The beauty glimmers with dawning gleams

At night the mystified stars that shone

The fireflies around her like magic spells

She gurgled with joy among the scented clump

With blossoming days, a maiden grown

With the rains came love from highland throne

A battered hero who saw no more

Than his love across the drizzling field

As if the heaven found his betrothed unknown

They found the love in the crystal showers

Where once she played and ran

The brooks had grown and bounty land

The clump brimming with flowers

They vowed when the drizzle adorn

The land breathed with joy

Of merry cheer and food and fest

That came to halt at the English horn

They found peace in thunder love in rain

They vowed on soul and joy

The horn blew a call of task

A battle story that brings pain and again

The sky weeped and weeped the whole day long

And several days more

Till battles fought that bled the grass

And bugle blew each darkness song

Came the king with spires in hand

Battles won, enemies gone

The realm is free, they told

But showering blisters didn't soothe her pain

Her love remain untold

They spoke no more of him and went

She ran across the field

It rained today amongst the corpse that lay

The blood the land appeared to yield

She found her vow and all her love

Battered and dunked in pain

Oh, my love, you belong to me

No matter the frame of crumbling pain

She found her joy in broken arms

And broken ribs that was never the same

But he who loved her bounty and more

And she would only love his claim

They danced in rain once more

A broken leg he came to fault

She picked him up and giggled again

For her life no more knew to halt.

With You

Often in the stealth of the night

When the moon shines bright

I walk the road I walked with you

The dawn of a morning

The half lit park

I stroll the park...I strolled with you

The dew laden bench

On a winter morning

A lazy finger rubs the dew

I smile the smile......I smiled with you

The hawker's tea

A steaming cup

The scent of the brew...a refreshment so

I quench the thirst....I quenched with you

The calm waters of the lake

Feet dipped in the nippy stretch

A playful splash..watching the ripples grow

I throat the giggle...I giggled with you

Now that you are blessed

An angel giggles at your hearth

A Bonnie smile ....a toddling fairy that makes you

smile

You smile with her .....I smile with you

Forever You Are Mine

The rains crept in the middle of the night.....

unearthly hours when I lay in your arms

A crooning melody plays in the background.....

the drizzle....the music...the panting rain.....

adds to the mood

Fingers entwining each other's.....

you know how mysteriously the gaps in mine fill

yours....

as if they were meant to hold them on such a

night

The breeze blows strands of hair on my face......

you raise your finger .....

do not touch the fateful face.....

it's for me to see and ponder upon.....

The fingers grow lightly on the skin....

taking it all the way back to my nape.....

a hand which stands comforting....

lessens the distance....

Eye meets the eye....

the breath so close to bear....

the lips seal in a silent kiss.....

beating and thumping the heart to tear

There are no knights in shining armor.....

but here you lay beside me motionless and still....

A breathing heart.....

love and care.....

tender touch and strong arms, fair.....

a protective embrace from you, my love

Even the damsels can't deny.....

not any knight...

or the mightiest king....

can embrace and sink in tranquil sleep ....

for you are ever mine.....

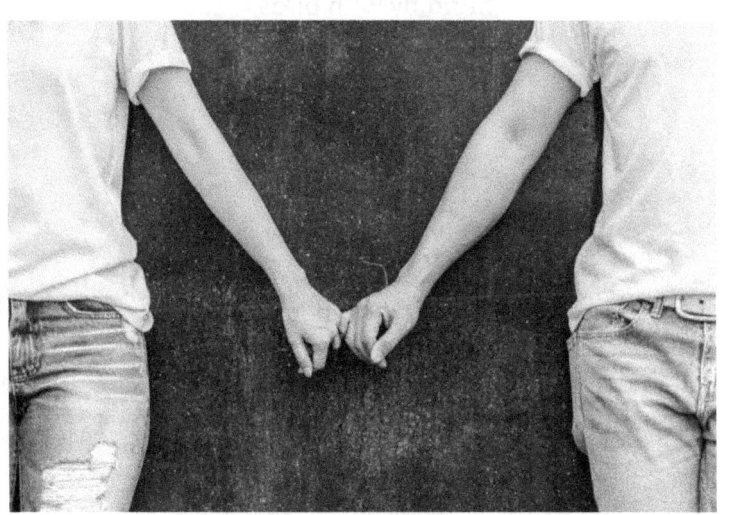

Woman As You Are

She was born to be free...

Among flowers and trees,

And fly with birds,

While playing with herds.

But shackles grew,

Before she knew,

For the lies they fed,

Of obscurity instead.

Her exuberance, shunted...

Her prowess, disregarded...

Her dreams, looted,

Her voice, muted.

Oh, people make way....

Of the new her today,

Of grace dignified,

And exuberance personified!

You hid her gift,

And thought they went adrift...

She was here always,

With absolute grace,

Amidst all shackles and ban,

Nurturing him to be a man.

She was a gem so rare,

You thought she was unaware...

Kept her locked,

While she taught you to walk.

Now think, oh, people.....

Whom you thought so feeble

Could bear the yolk and still be chaste

A man, so eternally penal....would he last?

An Absence In Chaos

"Jhoro jhoro borishe bari dhara

Hai pothobashi....Hai gotiheeno.....Hai grihohara"

-Rabindranath Tagore

It's been raining for three days now. What started as a surprise shower has brought back the losing spring chill into the air. While young and old argue about global warming over steaming mud cups of tea and bakery biscuits, some simply resort to the thrill of the wicked shiver of the downpour

Boshonto utsav being right around the corner, children are gearing up with the latest spray guns and Gariahat selling all the variable colors to add the galore of the much awaited Holi. The rain remains totally unaccounted for yet people seem glad. The deities receive happy, wholehearted head bows and prayers for the chills to last a little longer before the blasting summer turns the big bad goon and talk of the town.

It pours and pours. The clinking rain drops against the windows, the gushes on the road, the shed curtains of water making visibility a difficult proposition, the droplets ensuring cabbies dare lose their concentration while playing merrily on the windshield the "I make you sit on the edge" game.

Looking out the window the drops against the pane making various shapes of spiders, sliding against another to form a letter. slipping to join and make an animal, unmindful, I hum the lines.

A face makes a happy appearance and leaves with every blaring headlight illuminating the droplets into shining trinkets, a dazzle and gone!!! Again, the face among the faded darkness half lit, smiling,"Kemon acho?" A wicked taunting smirk that gorges into a throaty giggle.

Sitting here by the window, still recovering from the cold feet that the dirty cold water happily gulfed into my shoes. A steaming cup of tea, such a contrast against the pouring coolness against the steaming aromatic waves, each daring the other from the either side of the window glass and then, both suddenly conspiring to bring my favorite memory back, "Ki go chokotti?" and the throaty giggle. I smile aimlessly sipping on the steaming cup, embracing myself in an absent hug against a warm pot belly. "Boroder bhurite haat dite nei."

I laugh this time, blowing steam all over the

cup to form a cloud in the rain-cleared glass.

An unmindful finger simply scribbled childishly,

"Miss you......"

LA VIE MAGNIFIQUE

"I cannot rest from travel: I will drink

Life to the lees:"

-Ulysses, Lord Tennyson

She travelled with the wind and lay

Once upon a time in May

The sun kissed sand where they sang and say

Her love awaiting at the bay

They sang her song

They danced along

The flowers bloomed and birds tweet

Banquet of gourmet food and sweet

They drank and dined

The food and wine

With merry hearts of love

Till stars twinkled above

They lay on the warmth of sand

A far crooning of a weary band

The night with her mystic sky

Endless spirits of affections high

Her dazzling smile his gleaming eyes

The gorgeous splendor of love and surprise

The comfort of his arms around

The sumptuous softness of the ground

Her whispers of love

Of turtle dove

His endless smile

Charming and gentile

He knew he had this night with her

For leaving the shore to travel afar

The ships would sail at twilight dawn

And he would be gone to quest along

For months before he saw that smile

The gorgeous eyes like depths of Nile

His aching heart would quench and chime

As they lay embraced another time

A Golden Reward

Waiting for long when longing returns

The door ajar for you

You stride in oh, but casually

With memories old and new

I arise from my slumber embolden

From a silent wait that was golden.

For silence speaks what none hears

No fright no sound no beat

You came in silence to me from afar

No fear of renouncing or defeat

I arise from my slumber embolden

From a silent wait that was golden.

To love you when I was alone

Longed you more in solitude

You owned me with a smile

The heartiest the eyes can elude

I arise from my slumber embolden

From a silent wait that was golden.

The distance that held us apart

I chose to remain in love

For isolation knows no spurning

In the land, soul or above

I arise from my slumber embolden

From a silent wait that was golden.

You crept back when the rain set in

I kissed you when the sky sprinkled joy

For the droplets were gentler than my lips

Living my dreams in your arms employ

I arise from my slumber embolden

From a silent wait that was golden.

I dreamt the dreams even though distant

For my dreams held you to me

Forever and closest we were

Like the unbound endless sea

I arise from my slumber embolden

From a silent wait that was golden.

A Men Dream At Sea

"Peeping through the clouds of my bow

The bi-frost bridge appeared and how

Colours of heaven all but seven

Joy to my soul this rainbow has given"

-Capt Aditya Kale

Ahoy! Said the captain

To his unshakable crew

They marched into the nomadic sea

And bid the land adieu.

The boys will grow into men

The men would acquire stories

The treacherous sea awaits them

Where they carry forth their glories.

The mystic maiden voyaged along

To far off distant lands

With goods and tales to exchange

The oceans and seas they scanned.

They scourged many a land

For trades, where boys turn men

The calmness of the deeper sea

Grew treacherous calm again.

The night she came, an untamed tempest

From over a sudden creek

The frenzy crew the unshakable men

For a moment they felt weak.

Ahoy! Said the Captain

Shaking his locks of grey

She comes to test your zeal, your trust

Fear her not, beyond her we head our way.

Charge ! I say to the dooms door

Let her dance and torment

My men, I stand with you through her

tumultuous passion

For our zest to live is our sole consent.

We shall live with valor

And hold our pride

Come my lads with your souls of voyagers

Together let's break her tides.

The night long dance the tempest danced

The fury calmed and cool

The wary crew lay scattered and scarred

The mystic floated to Istanbul.

Ahoy! Said the captain

With a charge but cheer in his voice

Pointing to the distant sky

Where all men looked and rejoiced.

Said the Mogul with his locks of grey

Over the rainbow where the skies are blue

Your dreams, my men, that you dare to dream

They really do come true...

A Masterpiece

Have you seen the colors of spring

Rose, peach, orange, yellow, amber grease

Colors that I saw when Earth laughed with

flowers

To create a masterpiece

I yearn to touch the Autumn sky

Fluttering clouds on soothing blue that never

cease

Colours that I saw looking up at the blue

To create a masterpiece

The rains that pour across the glass

Reflect street lights with abundant release

Colours that I saw on rain stained glass

To create a masterpiece

The boyhood years of purling joys

Running across green moors, ever so peace

Colours that I saw at every meadow

To create a masterpiece

The church spires flame on a wedding day

Grooms and bride among-st laughter and bliss

Colours that I saw among-st their twinkling

eyes

To create a masterpiece

The August moon that shone of love

A soldier on his fence receives

Colours that I saw when he read his post

To create a masterpiece

Of all the colors in and around us

Our colourful world as we see

I am still to paint a picture for all

And create a masterpiece

A Soul Within

"I am not this hair

I am not this skin

I am this soul

that lives within"

- Rumi

Existence is pure Bliss.....

And to find it deep within

A gurgling child.....your mother's hand...

A white flower....the sea shore sand

A long warm hug.....a forgotten song

An old photograph hung all along

A toothless smile.....a quiet afternoon

A sudden rain.....a romantic moon

A lover's touch....a tinge of pain

A friend you lost.... and found again

A long, long ride....a scenic trip

A sailor's wind that moves his ship

The walk on grass....the wet cold dews

A box full of littering mews

A passionate kiss....a whisper in your ear

A sensuous touch of the skin so near

A tickle on skin....a glinting eye

The warmth of breath that takes you high

All that is worldly yet it is not

The universe and her powerful plot

To mesmerize the soul in you

Your identity....that you so knew......

Night Falls

The sun rises and sets in the blue

leaving a golden dust across the horizon

A twilight witnesses the dawn and dusk

But the night sky remains silent

The glory of the sun hides it all

with heat light and warmth

but the sky awaits

as patiently as the nocturnal soul

It rises again, silently yet beautifully

Spreading tiny specks of diamonds all across

her face

The crisp breeze pushing away the motionless

warmth

The land responds giving up the heat

Lying on the cool grass

resting my head on my arms

I smell the night

the coolness, the serenity, the calm comfort

Where she spreads her vast wings again

over me

over the entire cosmos

a black lyre studded with twinkling diamonds

Whispering in my ears as I doze off,

"He is still there

and i am watching over you both

Sleep my gentle .."

You Write. We Publish.

To publish your own book, contact us.

We publish poetry collections, short story collections, novellas and novels.

contact@thewriteorder.com

Instagram- @thewriteorder

www.facebook.com/thewriteorder

www.ingramcontent.com/pod-product-compliance
Lightning Source LLC
LaVergne TN
LVHW010428070526
838199LV00066B/5967